The A[...]
Liv[...] [...]appy L[...]

The Adventurer's Guide to Living a Happy Life

by Matt Mosteller

PREMIER
DIGITAL PUBLISHING

Premier Digital Publishing - Los Angeles

The Adventurer's Guide to Living a Happy Life

Copyright 2012 by Matt Mosteller

All rights reserved. Without limiting the rights under copyright reserved above, no part of this publication may be reproduced, stored in or introduced into a retrieval system, or transmitted, in any form, or by any means (electronic, mechanical, photocopying, recording, or otherwise) without the prior written permission of both the copyright owner and the above publisher of this book.

ISBN-13: 978-1-624670-09-1

ISBN-10: 1624670091

PREMIER
DIGITAL PUBLISHING

Published by Premier Digital Publishing

www.PremierDigitalPublishing.com

Follow us on Twitter @PDigitalPub

Follow us on Facebook: Premier Digital Publishing

PRAISE FOR MATT MOSTELLER'S BOOK:

* * * *

"When people ask me for tools to help them get their lives to work—tools to help them get out of their own way and find emotional freedom, I am often at a loss. I'm not a therapist, but I am a writer who wants to help people. Matt's powerful book, *The Adventurer's Guide to Living a Happy Life*, will be my go-to guide for positive living and I can't wait to share it with my readers."

Laura Munson, author of the international and New York Times best-selling book, This is not the Story you Think it is: A Season of Unlikely Happiness (Amy Einhorn/Putnam)

* * * *

"Matt Mosteller is the real deal when it comes to making a smile work in his favor. I have met few people who can maintain his level of positive thinking, even in the face of threatening situations that would daunt most others - whether those be in an office, atop a mountain, or faced with a Grizzly Bear. There are great lessons for anyone in this well-conceived little book."

Gordon Wiltsie. After more than 25 years leading and photographing expeditions to earth's wildest corners, Gordon Wiltsie has achieved international acclaim for his visual artistry. His work appears regularly in leading magazines such as National Geographic, Life, American Photo, Outside, National Geographic Adventure, Ski, Geo, and dozens of others. He also shoots on location for a broad mix of companies seeking creative, adventurous images for their products.

* * * *

DEDICATION

This book is dedicated to my family and friends, as I am fortunate to be on the receiving end of so much love, care, and inspiration from each and every one of you!

Don't let your life just follow a road. Get in your car and Drive Your Life to the fullest!

Take time to share your Life "Driving Lessons" with others as you don't know how important this is until someone who meant so much in your own life is gone.

* * * *

TABLE OF CONTENTS

1	Introduction	1
2	Fresh Beginnings	6
3	Physical Joy	10
4	Mental Prosperity	19
5	Emotional Purpose	31
6	Professional Development	40
7	Dream Attainment	48
8	Self Transformation	58
9	About the Author	74

* * * *

INTRODUCTION

There's no handbook for how to live our lives and not everyone has the opportunity to have an inspirational mentor who can provide us with honest and direct feedback that will move us in the right direction in life. When I was younger, I certainly felt like I was sailing without a rudder as my peers headed off to university, and I held onto my outdoor life of adventure. Many thought I was being foolish, that I wasn't following the right path to garner all the material trappings of life and the "traditional" view of what success was all about.

But something inside me, driving me like a cowboy herds stray cows, continued to push me further outside of the traditional path of life, further away from where my university buddies were going.

Over the course of twenty grueling years of adventures, I have more stories than I can count. From surviving a Grizzly attack, to climbing lonely summits, and skiing down uncharted steep and icy chutes, where one misstep meant certain death. In my youth I spent countless lonely nights sleeping in my car (in fact 63 nights one ski season, hence why there are 63 tips in this book!), running perilous rivers where others had perished and undertaking long journeys by foot through some of the most remote and rugged regions of North America.

More recently, I embarked on a multi-sport nightmare of an adventure across the Arctic Circle to some of the most northerly permanent settled villages. I spent days in the bone-chilling cold and shivering through nights in snow caves and tents where the only sounds you heard were tent poles snapping from the brutal cold, the clattering of your teeth like boxcars down a track and the wolves howling in anticipation of their next meal. I hoped it wasn't me.

My adventures have spanned land, water and over mountaintops. There was a time when my highly educated peers were convinced that my life compass was broken. I can see how they had their doubts–for a time I lived out of my car or couch surfed with friends and proudly claimed dirt floor digs of an early 1900s log cabin. I didn't have what many would consider the great comforts in life, but I gained a bank full of intuition, wisdom and experience in the process.

Since then, I've carved a career for myself in business that continues to combine my many passions. I do live a comfortable life now, but I still love to take on epic adventures which continue to define me today.

Through the pain of my many adventures, two beacons of hope have carried me forward—one is the complete and all-consuming power of a positive attitude, and the second is the amazing spirit you can gain from adding adventure to your life.

I found that adding adventure to my life could give me those "goose bump" moments that every human soul looks to find; the real zest of life that splits you from the mundane and that broadens your horizons as you make your way to new frontiers. With adventure we experience risks, hardships, incredible eye-opening wonders and experiences that can positively influence our lives. Adventure hones your basic instincts, enhances your senses, drives you to explore, gather food, walk the land and work with your clan to survive. It drives you to treat and interact with others with the utmost respect.

But no matter what you encounter in your daily life, you can't excel unless you have a positive attitude. Period. In the history of exploration and adventure, there is no example of long-term survival of an individual or team during times of incredible struggle or hardship that did not possess the basic skill of having immense amounts of optimism and positive energy.

Your attitude and approach to life truly can move mountains, get you jobs, inspire friendships and pick you up during your darkest moments. It's the key to having a wonderful life.

So how did I survive that Grizzly bear encounter? Below I have included daily tips that show how adventure can be an agent of positive change that will allow you to gain more "goose bump" moments in life and achieve things that up until now you have only dreamed about. Carpe diem!

* * * *

Attempting to run a marathon across the Arctic Circle — Yukon

* * * *

FRESH BEGINNINGS

1. Start Your Day Smart

Choose your view and your attitude from the start of the day. Undoubtedly you have encountered a person at work who just looks like a troll–grim and grumpy from the start of the day onward. Make it your intention to start each day with a fresh outlook. Don't carry a burden over from a bad meeting or a mistake that was made. Learn from it and move on.

As we walk down our daily paths, we are constantly bombarded by negative thoughts– from ourselves and others. These thoughts impede our ability to truly get the most out of life. We all have speed bumps–whether it's getting frustrated, waiting on the phone for technical support to issues related to marriage, family and work. It is how we face these challenges that make a difference.

You have two choices—let it bog you down or move wisely to find a solution. When a negative thought enters your mind, replace it with a positive one and focus on creating a solution to the problem at hand. It's the old adage that the "glass is half full" —those with an optimistic, positive attitude tend to go further in life.

* * * *

2. Start Your Day Early

Start your day early if you want to be productive in life, even if you need a crutch like strong French roast coffee. I start my day at 4:30 a.m.—it's not something that everyone can do. Do what you can and make the time your own. The key is to make time to find energy for your day. An early morning start can help you get engaged and productive on projects which will make a difference in the outcome and productivity of your entire day.

* * * *

3. Get Engaged

You can either be in the bleachers as a spectator of life or you can be on the field. This is a life choice that you have to make over and over again in life, and many people struggle with these decisions. It is much easier to sit in the bleachers, and it takes work, risk and an element of discomfort to be in the game.

* * * *

4. Get in the Game Everyday

Staying on task and on track is never easy. Doing this day in and day out is downright difficult. Whether it's your passion, your job or your work, commitment is challenging. It doesn't matter if you sell cars, produce works of art or trade stocks; it is easy to give yourself an excuse. There's always that little voice in your head that says, "Don't make that difficult call", or "Don't go on that run today". Don't give in. Make a schedule and stick with it. Ultimately procrastination is more challenging than just getting the task done.

I'm from the Land of Hockey, where we say, "You can't score if you're not in the game". Get in the game. Don't accept no for an answer or let criticism get in your way. I have a confession to make–it has taken me at least 10 years to write this short book. Only until I made myself work on it every day was I able to complete it. Writing for me is hard and every project has its setbacks. You have to know you are not alone and you're not the first person to have hardship working on a passion, project, art or dream. Stick to your schedule, work on it each day and don't let anyone kick you out of the game.

* * * *

THE ADVENTURER'S GUIDE TO LIVING A HAPPY LIFE

Exploring the mountain world one journey at a time

* * * *

PHYSICAL JOY

5. Create Your Adventure Activity

One of the best ways to create more positivity in your life is to set an adventure goal that you can focus on and that will provide you with a daily challenge. For me, preparing for the Yukon Challenge provided a daily "Positive Explosion", as it gave me a major challenge to prepare for each day.

Your own adventure can be simple or challenging. It can be for a day, week, month or a year. I recommend starting off with setting up some Weekly Adventures. It could be a walk in a local park, a canoe in a nearby lake, a snowshoe across the field, downhill skiing or snowboarding in your local area or trying cross-country skiing. Depending on where you live, many of these sports have local shops or clubs that can provide resources for getting started.

* * * *

6. Heart Pump for Brain Power

There is more to exercise than sweating and looking at yourself in the mirror at a health club…it makes you smarter. Many studies show students who exercise regularly and who are physically fit get better grades in school. In fact, the students who were in the best shape also had the best average scores overall. Make exercise a part of your day and get on a plan. There are many easy plans on the market now that complement technology that you likely already have at home. For example, you can set up a running application on your iPod or similar device and build a program to suit your needs and help you to achieve your goals. With so many programs available, excuses such as "I can't afford a trainer" or "I don't know where to start" can't be accepted anymore. I used one of the applications to set up a simple sixty-five day training program to prepare for the Yukon Challenge Half Marathon.

'Active Living Research, Physical Activity and Academic performance', Stewart G. Trost, PHD. Fall 2007

'California Journal of Health Promotion' an evaluation of the relationship between Academic Performance and Physical Fitness measures in California Schools, Sangeeta Singh, June 2006

* * * *

7. Smile Ultimately

I firmly believe that it is our responsibility in life to make someone's day, each and every day. A simple way to do this is to smile–smile often and genuinely. It will not only make you feel good; it will make someone else's day.

* * * *

8. Expand Yourself- Physically and Mentally

Less than fifty days now until the Yukon Challenge, the world's toughest winter adventure race. We are doing this race with only sixty-five days of training. Why? It's the question I get all the time. But I am convinced that you need to push yourself out of your comfort zone, do different things and do things you have never done before to grow. Expand yourself both physically and mentally. Reach out beyond your normal routine. In order to grow and develop your skills and mind, you need to push into new territory. This event is a real push for me. I'm not the guy you see out in the neighbourhood running in spandex or biking every day.

I have lead an active outdoor life. I love the outdoors and spending time in nature. But I'm certainly not your typical cardio athlete.

I know from past experience that every time you do an extraordinary adventure, you grow. It doesn't have to be the world's toughest winter adventure race or even a forty mile hike in a day, but do something that pushes your limits in your world. For example, you may have always wanted to go on a sailing adventure. What does that adventure entail? You will need to take sailing classes, navigation classes and get some experience on a sailing boat. Before you know it, you can be the captain of your own sailboat and enjoy an amazing adventure. This is just one example of many you could dream up. It could be a Kenya safari, or a backpacking trip in your local wilderness. There are endless examples of what you can do in your own backyard or around the world that can help push your limits and expand your horizons.

How do you benefit from the adventure? There are the steps that you take as you prepare yourself and plan your challenge and the accompanying milestones that you focus on along the way. Once the actual task is at hand, there's a charge of anticipation and energy and your increasing confidence when you realize you will achieve your goal after much preparation and discipline.

Your real growth happens when you take the time to reflect on your accomplishment and learn from it. Reflection provides inner strength when you recognize that you have proven to yourself that you are able to do something that you didn't think you could do. This is very powerful for your inner self-esteem and is a powerful charge of confidence.

You've benefitted in so many ways—you've expanded your skill sets and your mental power. Now you have this inner strength to reflect on it and to draw from it in other facets of your life in the future. For example, you may find yourself in a challenging work situation and you can draw from "If I can withstand being in bitter cold temperatures and frozen to the core, then I can accomplish what's in front of me now".

Adventure allows you to learn about yourself in situations that are not normal. Your adventure provides you with physical growth; perhaps you will have challenged yourself with some situations that require athletic skills: building balance, cardio and agility. Then there's the mental side–you will have exercised your ability to slay negative thoughts and doubts that try to cripple your ability to accomplish your goal. On the mental side you will have taken huge steps forward in terms of how you approach life and its accompanying challenges.

* * * *

9. Push Your Comfort Zone and Find Your Passion

Expose yourself to a wide variety of activities, interests and projects to find your true passions. Don't fret about this. Drive yourself to try a number of different things. Do something that scares you or makes you feel anxious. Put yourself in different shoes to find your true passions.

Never limit yourself and find ways to deal with the things that make you scared. I have had bouts where I have been terrified of flying. When the cabin door closes, I get a wave of apprehension that I am trapped or that I'm not in control. I immediately engage in deep breathing and sometimes I even pinch my ear. The breathing helps to relax me and pinching the ear? It may seem strange, but the sharp pain makes me snap out of my negative thought pattern and replace it with more positive thoughts.

Whether it's sport, travel, education or setting your own personal challenge, do what scares you and find your passion.

* * * *

10. Stimulate Your Mind Through Sport

Take time each day to do a run, walk, hike, workout, yoga, or whatever it is you love that gets you moving for at least 30 minutes each day. In addition to the well documented health benefits, this will also give you a daily hit of exercise-induced endorphins. Endorphins are a great miracle cure in your life. We have the power to heal ourselves in so many ways simply by getting daily exercise. Endorphins can help provide us clarity to make better decisions and provide peace to our system and help make your body stronger by giving your immune system a boost.

'Scientists Hint at Why Laughter Feels So Good' James Gorman, New York Times Sept 13th 2011

* * * *

11. Make a Commitment to Your Higher Purpose

Have a concrete purpose. This will help you to navigate through tough times. We all face challenges regularly but maintaining a positive attitude and a higher purpose will provide the internal strength to make it through any challenge presented.

Your higher purpose can take a variety of forms. It could be your commitment to care and provide for your family, to assisting a friend with cancer or achieving a goal in a sport or activity that you have set for yourself.

When I set the goal that I was going to enter the world's toughest winter adventure race, I had no idea how tough the training would be, how bad the local weather conditions for training would be and how tough it is to make time to train when you have a full-time job and a busy family life.

But my wife and I dug in and found ways to stay committed to our goal. We changed our morning routine, allowing me time to work, write and then get in a workout all before the kids got out of bed. So, I started my day between 4:30 a.m. and 5 a.m. This certainly did have an impact on my bedtime. I am now, as the kids say, "a party pooper". But I feel that I have much more energy, vitality and am more engaged due to achieving a more restful sleep thanks to maintaining a very healthy diet and getting in my daily workouts. But it's so easy to get knocked off the tracks. Given that I have a very busy hosting and social schedule with my work, it can be tougher some weeks than others to keep up with my routine. But like anyone human I try my best. If I miss a day, then I try to make it a "Rest Day" in the training cycle and pick up on the next day of my regular routine.

Don't stress yourself out about missing days here and there. The key is to try and be consistent over time and to stick to a regular program the best that you can. Sleep, diet and exercise are all key to help keep you on track.

* * * *

12. Too Tired to Triumph

Now for the opposite of that last tip and it's an important one. Sometimes you feel tired and it can be hard to get engaged. Take a few steps back. Take a nap. If you can't take a nap, recharge, then step back and reflect on what you are doing. Take a few deep belly breaths and stir your mind on what matters and what's challenging you. Maintain your focus on your goal.

So, to stay fresh you have to build some rest periods into your routine. Stay on track with regular sleep hours and go to bed and wake up at consistent times. Do everything you can to keep yourself on track and listen to what your mind and body requires to perform at its best. Make rest part of your routine and it will help give you the energy you need in your training regime.

* * * *

Enjoying adventures with friends and family

* * * *

MENTAL PROSPERITY

13. Nature Provides Benefits

Get out and explore. Take a walk through a park you have never visited or read a guide book. Get online and research local hikes, and choose one that fits your interest. Today, more people than ever are becoming less connected with nature. Cities have little green space and people forget the renewal powers of nature. This is affecting society on many levels.

Nature provides a place like no other to relax. Nature is an excellent natural cure to help keep stress and anxiety at bay. Seek out the mountains, a nature park or visit a favourite lake. Being in nature also helps to enhance your senses—each one gets more attuned as you spend time in the great outdoors. It's the delectable taste of trailside blackberries (just select your berries carefully), to listening to squirrels rustling through leaves or the wind in the trees. Nature heals.

* * * *

14. I am a Sleep Crusader

Despite getting up early each day, I am a sleep crusader. My kids think I am nuts for going to bed before them but there is a background to my sleep crusade. Here are some tips I have to ensure a good, restful sleep:

Don't work out before bedtime. I believe in the power and benefit of exercise, but just don't do it within 3 or 4 hours of your bedtime. You are revving up your heart and mind just as you are trying to shut down systems for relaxation and sleep time.

Don't eat big meals before bedtime. Your stomach does not need this type of workout before bed, and it will keep you up. Also, you will achieve better digestion if you eat more times throughout the day. Not just three full meal times but good high quality nutritious food spread out between four to six eating times.

Don't get your mind too engaged before bedtime. Don't review work or other subjects that could charge you up. Leave these active tasks to your early morning regime. Get to bed at the same time each night. Get into a routine. As an adult, get eight hours of sleep per night. Sleep is a brain fuel, it helps to recharge your system and strengthen your immune system.

Consider meditating and relaxing before you go to sleep. A simple deep breathing exercise can calm the mind and nervous system so you can relax and go to sleep. Breathe in five seconds through your nose and exhale five seconds through your mouth. Do it in a slow and methodical way and focus on listening to the sound of your breath. Also feel your stomach rise and then flatten out with the exhale to help clear stale air from your body.

'Highlighting the positive impact of increasing feeding frequency on metabolism and weight management' Louis Sylvestre J, 2003

* * * *

15. Dance Nude, Sing and Play Games

What is this all about? Make it a point to have crazy, unreasonable fun every day. Make fun a part of your day and in everything you do. Push your limits with fun as well to stimulate self-esteem and deep belly laughs. Like many, you may be afraid to dance nude. Now it could be that you didn't want others to see your body, or you may have self-esteem or self-awareness issues. But in order to start pushing these mind limits away, you need to face them. Take your clothes off and dance until you can't dance anymore. Look at yourself in the mirror and be happy. Say positive words about yourself.

Sing in the shower if you are afraid to sing in public. Work your way up—next. Sing in the living room. Then sing in your front yard and from there you'll find that you can sing wherever and whenever you want. Don't limit yourself by worrying about what others think about you. Expand your horizons by doing fun and different things and having full belly laughs along the way. Everyone wants to hang with people that are having fun and who are comfortable with themselves.

* * * *

16. Act Like a Baby

There's something that (almost) all babies do really well and that we should all be doing. And that's napping. Short (ten to fifteen minute) naps are great. They help you to relax, recharge your batteries and keep going. Short naps, combined with highly nutritious food is a sure bet for keeping your energy levels strong and giving you a strong foundation for success.

* * * *

17. Everything We Think Upstairs Effects What's Going to Happen Downstairs

The mind dictates how you perform. Even if you are the world's best athlete, you can be knocked out of a competition by your mind. For example, a basketball player who misses a key shot and then dwells on that poor shot can have his skills hampered by that negativity and lack of confidence. Recognize that this can happen and then figure out your best way of moving on after you've had a poor performance, either at work or in sport.

Incidents occur every day that you could get caught up in: one of your accounts could decide not to renew if you are in sales, or your company could receive some negative press about a new product you have been working on. In these situations, tell your mind to move forward and replace your negative thoughts with something positive. Then, work hard to define positive steps forward from the situation. Not only will your staff and office appreciate that you are looking at positive ways to improve the situation but you will also be able to deliver a better product.

Adventures are good at helping you learn and apply this skill. The unexpected always happens when you are adventuring, and it can be detrimental to your wellbeing and safety if you dwell on negative situations during a long backpack trip or canoe voyage.

One trip that I took involved a 40 mile hike in one day. The distance was far, and it involved having to cross a high mountain pass, coupled with midday temperatures over 90 degrees Fahrenheit. The heat, lack of drinkable water and a very long hike contributed to many low points along the way. It would have been easy to give in and rest longer but we needed to arrive at our campsite before nightfall. We focused on having a "move forward" mindset, and the one way we did that was through humor. Be humble enough to be able to laugh at yourself and your situation, and then use that burst of energy to keep going forward. Channel positive thoughts faster than the negative thoughts can come into your mind. Make up small goals to keep moving forward. You can say to yourself: "just to that next tree or ridge" and so on. Don't worry as much about your pace, as it is about positive progress. Take small steps forward through small goals, and before you know it you will be there. They say that "Life is full of setbacks". Your success is often determined by how you overcome setbacks.

* * * *

18. Trust More

It is just as important to be trusting of others as it is to be trustworthy. On many occasions we hear stories and details from friends and co-workers and as they are telling us their stories, doubts or disbelief begins to surface. In order to build that strong bond with your families, co-workers and friends, you need to establish trust. Always trust first, until proven differently. This is easy to say but can be very hard to do in practice. It is critical that a high level of trust exists in your family. Your kids easily feed on a trusting bond, but this can go the other direction with doubt and fear taking over if the trust net is not strong. This is a key part of the child foundation of strength, as self-esteem is formed by this trust net. Children need to learn to tell the truth and that you will always believe them, no matter the situation. You will feel much better about yourself and those around you with a strong trust net cast, then you don't have to second guess, worry or concern yourself with doubt.

Walk in trust more with each step of your day. This morning, I have to place trust in my footing with each step as there are icy patches in the darkness of the morning. I will place trust in my balance skills and footing is key to a safe and strong winter run. Trust in your daily life is important for strong lasting friendships and is a critical element of a strong positive family.

* * * *

19. Add Some Seuss to Your Life

A family favorite for us is "The Grinch Who Stole Christmas". The little girl who is the star of this family classic is a glowing reminder that the power of positive belief can make a difference. She never wavers in her positive attitude even in the face of harsh criticism from everyone in "Whoville". We all need to add a little Seuss to our lives.

The Seuss of positive belief is in one's self. Don't waver in having a positive attitude when all your co-workers are negative or don't agree with your input. Have a strong conviction for what you believe in and you will carve a positive path in your life. In the end, the young Seuss star was right and her positivity helped to transform the entire town of Whoville.

* * * *

20. There is Good in Taking Time to Reflect

In the ebb and flow of your busy days, it's important to take the time to review and reflect, at least on a daily basis. When I had a limited amount of time to prepare for the Yukon Challenge, we ensured that we took days off from working out and running so that our muscles and bodies would have time to repair and rebuild.

Our minds and spirits also need some down time. Build in this time every day so that you can reflect on the key items you want to get done that day and also make adjustments to your action list so that you can stay on track. In business, take a moment for yourself prior to a meeting to review your agenda and prepare your thoughts. Allowing time to reflect will help you refocus, generate new ideas and bring calm to your world.

* * * *

21. Sometimes Your Brain Tries to Limit Your Gain

One morning, I was on a seven mile training run in cold temperatures along Calgary's Bow River with a frosty wind blanketing my face and creating a burning pain in my frozen hands. My mind kept telling me to stop, to head back earlier than I had set out to do. We all have two negatives working against us in our daily lives—one is our mind (or body) telling us no and the other is the limiting thoughts from others about our abilities.

In this particular situation, I stayed the course. I put some more upbeat music on and told myself to carry on, one step at a time.

Now, I should explain that if you are risking creating or aggravating an injury then you have to listen to your body and know when to stop. But when your body is in fine form and your mind is telling you to stop because you are uncomfortable, that's when you need to recognize what your mind is telling you and know when to push on.

When you are working towards your fitness goal (or any goal for that matter), every day of training is vital to achieving your goal. You have to believe that every step is critical to achieving your greatness. You have to dig deep to find simple ways of turning your pain, doubts or yearning to stop into the drive to continue on.

When it comes to workouts, I break down my exercise into little steps when the going gets tough. I take it literally one minute at a time. I get through that minute, and then go to the next and so on and so forth. In no time you will have completed that last 15 minutes. You can also add some music or get a training companion to pump you up.

Change your mind's view if you can. Switch to other subjects to think about and before you know it you will have completed your training. Think of the pain as your muscles gain. Every bit of training will make you stronger and better able to attain your goal. It's always easy to stop (or not start at all) but this won't get you any further ahead. Know your body and train safely and within your means but don't get scared about pushing your limits. You never know how far you can go until you get there.

The other component that can have a negative impact on you is when others start telling you negative opinions and creating self-doubt within yourself. You only have one person you need to listen to and that person is you. Convert the doubter's thoughts into positive energy that helps fuel your drive.

I have always been charged up by people who tell me that I can't do something. It immediately makes me want to prove them wrong. But make sure that whatever you take on fits into your core passions and that you aren't just doing things to prove others wrong. Do it for you! It becomes much more powerful when you find your passion and let that fuel your drive. Tune out negative thought, whether it comes from others or is created in your own mind.

People have a tendency to be negative. From the mental strength you have gained, always reflect on the positive and keep your momentum going.

* * * *

22. Anxiety – Hard to Spell and Even Harder to Deal With

Anxiety–you are not alone. All of us have some form of it. It comes in all shapes, colors and fashions. None of us are fans of anxiety, but the quicker you realize that you have some form of it, the better you will be. Don't let it rule your life. Get aggressive with it and find ways that you can manage it, diminish it or make it go away completely from your life.

Some common anxieties include a form of fear: fear of heights, fear of tight spaces, a fear of performance. It has many forms. Fear of flying is a favorite one. Now, I'm not a medical professional in any way, shape or form to give you advice on this. I can only offer my simple input. I have experienced and have various forms of anxieties or panic attacks. In the beginning, I had no clue what they were and I brushed them off. When they became more frequent, I began to worry and wondered what they were.

Was something completely wrong with me? Did I have some sort of strange medical issue? Sweat would break out when I had to give a big speech and my words and lines would get bunched up, or I would forget words.

I felt very anxious when I got onto airplanes, particularly when they closed the cabin door. I felt helpless. I had to get a grip. I realized from many discussions with very successful people that all of these feelings, all of these panic attacks and performance anxieties were normal. I was not the only one who experienced this, and you are not the only one who experiences this. You are normal. Once you recognize this, then focus on finding simple solutions to dealing with anxiety when it occurs. Then determine some relaxation or meditation techniques that work for you. Breathing helps to calm the mind and body.

The key is finding simple solutions–whether you try my "pinch the ear lobe" trick to help refocus your energy or engaging your mind on something else–figure out what will help you deal with your anxiety. Recognize when you are facing a challenging experience and then use your strong mental will power to overcome it. Each time it will become easier–trust me!

* * * *

23. You Can Lead a Horse to Water, but You Can't Make it Drink

Your friend will not call you back. Your husband or partner's actions are bothering you. Your son's friend is not responding to a text message he sent him for the 30th time, and this is really eating him up.

Every day, we have situations we face or things that happen to us that affect us. Wondering or worrying about the actions of others, or the thoughts that they have towards you can eat you up inside. Asking why something is or isn't, is not doing something.

You need to step back and let this worry slide on by, as you focus on what you can control. You can't control the actions of others but you can focus on your own actions.

Now, this isn't easy but next time you have this happen to you, start by doing one action to get your mind focused on the positive. Help a friend out, shovel the snow from their driveway, cook a meal for an elderly neighbour, or assist your son or daughter with their homework. Do something for you. Work on your book, start an art project, read a blog on a topic of interest, go to the library, go out for a walk, or try something new but don't waste your time worrying about what others may or may not be thinking about you.

* * * *

EMOTIONAL PURPOSE

24. Passion

Become a passion for you. I am convinced that having passions is a key element in life. Having adventure passions enhance your health (mental and physical benefit from the activity), enhance your social life and ignite your spirit. You can have a number of passions. Uncover what you love and pursue goals that are aligned with your passions.

* * * *

25. Adore More

Many of my training and preparation days for the Yukon challenge were done in miserable weather. One specific training day started off on a snowy early winter day. As I prepared for my run I sat down with our golden retriever

Maverick, listening to the wind howl. Not sure that I wanted to venture out into the heart of a prairie snowstorm, I was strengthened by the unconditional love from Maverick. Sharing your love with your dog, your friends and your family is the cornerstone of life. Do this daily.

It can be as simple as leaving a note that says "I Love You" on your partner or kids' beds, or daily hugs. Share your adoration for those you love every day. Share kisses and compliments and go the extra step to find the good in each person.

Share positive comments or highlight something that person did that made you feel happy, proud or impressed. Also, focus on taking your relationship with your partner to deeper levels both physically and emotionally.

* * * *

26. A Positive Purpose

Whether your work is your passion or simply how you make a living, everyone has to deal with work in one way or another. Regardless of the situation, how you approach your work and the people around you impacts who you are and how you perform. One way is to "Greet and Engage"–have a positive discussion with everyone you come into contact with at your work.

Over a period of time, you will create a positive mindset for yourself, as well as a positive impression in the minds of others. Positive creates positive, and people are attracted to positive people around them. Even if you come across pessimistic types–talking about how they got up late (so tired), complain about the weather (so gray), or fought through traffic to work (so slow). Stay true to your positivity, and it may change their attitude too.

If you're not doing what you're passionate about, it's never too late to make a change–start your passion now. Make it a point to make each day beautiful for you and for others around you. Never forget–a smile can go a very long way.

* * * *

27. Face-Off With Fear

You see many successful people in various situations. These successful CEOs, entrepreneurs and business owners do many daily tasks. Some you see on the front line assisting their cashiers with cash out, some cleaning the factory floor with the team, some redesigning the assembly line and so on. One important element these leaders all share is that they had a "Face-off with Fear". They challenged themselves to do the things that most of us would put off doing. Why do we put it off? It's because we are scared to do it or don't believe that we can do it.

You need to have your own Face-off with Fear to deal with the things you believe you can't do. You may have fear of dealing with the bank on a loan, or a fear of dealing with unhappy guests after an experience with a product you made. You may have a fear of confronting a family member about a problem they may have or having a difficult conversation with a partner or friend. It's time to Face-off with your fear. First, define the items or actions that create this feeling. Then jump into action and face your fear head on. You will likely find that the action of worrying was greater than actually dealing with the situation itself. You will amaze yourself with what you can accomplish. Jump into the game to "Face-off" with your fears and move forward.

* * * *

28. Happiness– Enjoy Each Minute of the Day

The old adage of enjoying each step of your journey is right! If you are going to be successful, it is critical that you become happy right here and now in whatever situation you may find yourself. You may have thoughts of "I am not in the best job right now" or "This isn't where I want to be living" etc. As you work towards a positive change or solution that will work for you, enjoy your current situation and make the most of it.

If you constantly believe that you will be happier doing something or being someone else, then you will never find true happiness. It takes time and energy to change each moment into a positive one. You will benefit if you change your frame of mind to focus on the present. Turn every step into a positive, and every time your mind races ahead thinking it will be better further ahead–stop it! Create a laughing moment with a prank or a joke and relish in that time. See what you are doing through a kid's perspective so that you are always seeing with anticipation or excitement. Or, if you are doing the same routine over and over, seek a new angle or new perspective on what you are doing.

Further, look at ways to enhance your experiences so it makes a difference in someone else's life. Doing well for someone else can really change your own feelings and attitude. I can share an example from my early days of skiing. I had a great opportunity to participate in some of the early classic cult ski films (think Warren Miller). I was really pumped and headed out to take on this opportunity. However, my mind was elsewhere. I kept thinking about a girlfriend I had at the time, as she was trying to figure out if I was right for her or not. Thinking about my personal situation kept eating away at me, and I couldn't give my all for the ski film. In the end, I returned home and within a week we broke up. My fretting while taking away focus from the present moment ended up being a total waste of time. You need to be exactly where you are—only then you will find peace, happiness and the ability to give your all to whatever you are working on.

* * * *

29. Set Your "Happy Bar" High

I review each of my "must-have" items in preparation for my run at 5:30 a.m. in the morning. Banana? Check. Coffee? Check. Steel cut oats? Check. Dog? Wait. The dog isn't ready. He's flopped out on the family couch snoring away. He is always slow to get up for me because I don't provide him his sole motivation in life—food. My wife feeds him and gets all of the accompanying attention and adoration. He listens for any movement from upstairs in the mornings–he knows the sound of her steps and only stirs when he hears them. I try to wrestle him up with words like "walk" and "run" to see if can get any action from him. But nothing is working. So I stir the food bin and see him perk up a bit but he's still glued to the couch. I get my coffee and sit down next to him. He suckers me in to giving him a full body rub but at least now I have got his attention. Before I know it his ear is in my coffee and his tongue is on my face and he's licking me with the same zest a kid puts into an ice cream cone.

Sometimes happiness needs to be pushed. Focus on what makes you happy and what you can do to stir happiness and bring happiness into your life regularly. Make it part of your adventure. In the same way that you are planning to bring adventure into your life to grow and inspire yourself, make happiness part of your own adventure.

How do you do this? Focus on your happy moment and spend time with people who you think are fun. Once you start to have more happiness in your life, more will come your way and your happy bar will be raised.

* * * *

30. Random Acts of Kindness

Doing good for others helps others but it also helps you. Add a positive boost to each day by doing simple acts of random kindness every day. Open the door for someone, say hello to a stranger, shovel the sidewalk for a neighbor you have never met, help an older person with their grocery bags to the car. There are endless examples of how you can share kindness with others.

* * * *

31. Be a Connector

Every day you come into contact with people. Learn more about them; be interested in what they do or what they have to say. Learn something from each contact you make. I try to ask lots of questions since everyone has an interesting story about themselves or their passions. People love to be asked to talk about themselves, and people love to be connected.

In business, be sure you follow up with people after a meeting and share something that they imparted on you during that meeting. Perhaps connect them with another person who might be able to help them in their pursuit or who you think have similar interests to them. It can be as simple as recommending a book for them based on what you know about them. Get connected and then connect others; the benefits will return to you in spades.

* * * *

32. Fear and Doubt Are Great Motivators

If you lead an adventure-filled life, you will most certainly have both Fear and Doubt as close friends at many points along the way. It is critical to recognize these daily motivators in your routine.

On many adventures, you can have some of your best growth opportunities happen in the most fearful situations. You can also make the most progress in life and work being driven by fear.

Going way back to caveman times, both Fear and Doubt have been our best drivers. When you hear the bone-chilling screech of a mountain lion or have a bear sighting in the woods, you are immediately pumped up with adrenaline and invoke your life-saving mode of flight. You have to channel this fear.

When in the wild with every one of these situations, you come back with incredible memories and also growth. Knowing and trusting that you are able to deal with these adversities and that you will survive will transform you into a more confident decision maker.

In day-to-day work or family life, you may not have to deal with a mountain lion or bear on a regular basis, but you do have to make decisions that others won't dare to do. Believe in your skills and abilities. Do your homework thoroughly and just go for it.

Just like fear, people don't like doubt. But this uncertainty is the state that provides you with the most creative and innovative thoughts. You need uncertainty to stimulate your senses so you can create your art in life. Don't get stifled and just settle for the most comfortable situation or solution. Push the envelope, drive into uncertain situations and relish in the growth and energy these challenges can provide you.

* * * *

33. Love the Ones You're With

We have been very fortunate to escape to the no frills, classic mountain cabin built in the 1950s and perched high in the Rocky Mountains. Usually when we arrive, it takes at least a full day for it to heat up. You walk briskly around as you see your breath and the temperature inside feels colder than the temperature outside. But this place is full of a different kind of warmth.

The cabin gets us all disconnected from regular life and allows us to unplug our electronic gadgets (yes, no internet!) and the only electronic device is one that my kids can't even recognize and plays classic country Christmas music. This is a place where you have tradition, where you work together and where you share stories. We go out and cut down our own Christmas tree, and each of us has a task that we are responsible for.

My son handles the logging and carrying the tree back, while our golden retriever tries to grab the stick end to chew on it. My daughter is the designer and has the eyes to see beauty in anything. My wife and I sing Christmas songs (she very well and me quite poorly) as we sit and watch the kids decorate the tree with Christmas cheer.

Find your special place that brings your friends and family close together and share traditions with them. While you sit there enjoying these special moments, you can never say these three words enough: "I Love You". Say them over and over to your kids, spouse, parents and close friends.

* * * *

PROFESSIONAL DEVELOPMENT

34. What's Your Gig?

When we were young, everyone started out dreaming of being a policeman, firefighter, airline pilot, movie star or singer, etc. What happened? Most of us got sidetracked. We got jobs. But did you get your dream job? Most likely not–you did what your friends, parents, or what you told yourself you should do. No matter what you do (or didn't do), it's never too late to pursue some of your childhood dreams.

If you start subscribing to earlier mornings, you can use that time to consider the job of your dreams and build your skills. If you want to be a singer, start singing in the morning! Always wanted to be a stockbroker? Open an online account and start trading. Whatever your dream job, take some steps towards it as part of your morning routine. It doesn't mean you have to give up your current job–invest time and energy into yourself and your passions and start making steps towards what you want to do in your life.

Inquire with your employer to see if there are education dollars available to build your skills and add to your pursuits while benefitting your employer. For example, if you work at an engineering firm but want to get into Marketing or Social Media, approach your employer about taking relevant courses in that field and then suggest creating a blog for the company or working with the marketing department on some of their initiatives. This will help you explore other areas, build your skills, while continuing to add value to the organization you work for.

Most companies have programs in place to support staff education. Education is never a waste. It will help you get the skills that will benefit you while exploring options to do what you want to do.

Taking on a new skill or contemplating a possible career change has its elements of risk. Risk can be frightening and can leave doubt in your mind. What will your parents think? Your spouse? Will your friends laugh at you? Taking a leap is never easy. Convert your negative thoughts of "I can't" to "I will". "I will" is much stronger than "I can" because it is positive direct action.

If you are striving towards a goal–just sign yourself up. Whether it's for an educational course at your local university or college, or committing to running that first half-marathon, saying "yes" is easier than coming up with the hundred reasons why you could say "no".

When I first heard of the Yukon Challenge, I learned that running a half marathon was just one of the ten events taking place over ten days. At the time, I couldn't run more than four miles, and even then it was at a very slow pace. Add to that the additional challenge of doing such a race in frigid temperatures that could near minus 40 degrees Celsius; "I can't" was a natural reaction.

However signing up gave me the nudge to start training, and once you start, the rest (with hard work and dedication) falls into place. Just starting and instead of talking makes all the difference for your adventure. The key is not to listen to the negative and sign up. Make the commitment and get in the game.

* * * *

35. See and Learn How Others Excel

Focus on people's strengths. You will go further and gain more benefit if you focus on people's strengths. Everyone wants to be appreciated. Your friends, co-workers and partner will greatly appreciate you if you highlight their strengths and show them you value them for what they offer. But another benefit is that you can learn from them and enhance your own skills.

I have a friend who is a natural public speaker. He can stand up in front of a crowd of any size and his words just flow, and he is able to engage the entire crowd. After one of his recent speaking engagements, I gave him a compliment about his positive skills as a public speaker. I asked him if he could provide me any of his tips. He thanked me for recognizing this skill and because of my appreciation and friendship he also provided me some key tips that I have used to enhance my own public speaking skills.

* * * *

36. Do the Unexpected

When we set out to do the Yukon Challenge, we had no idea what we were getting ourselves into. We wouldn't be thought of as the normal types of people to do such an event since we had not even run a 10km event before, which is a normal everyday type of event for most adventure racers or running enthusiasts. Do the unexpected in life to not only change your view and challenge yourself but also to be different. Go out each day with eyes and ears searching out ways to be different and to stand out. Doing the unexpected challenges yourself and creates a special way for you to set yourself apart from everyone else.

* * * *

37. Pay Attention to Each Step

Don't overlook the importance of each step. Creating the framework for a successful foundation in life is all in the details. You may blow off bringing water on a run, thinking you're not thirsty but suddenly the weather changes, and it becomes hotter than usual, and your body starts screaming for liquid. For a basketball player, practicing a foul shot has to become part of their routine each and every day. Dedication to practice and instilling focus might be what makes or breaks the shot on game day.

When you set yourself in motion to achieve success, you need to make sure you pay attention to each step along the way. Similarly in business, you must account for every dollar spent or you risk going out of business. Each and every penny counts in life. And remember, small change can add up to big rewards.

* * * *

38. Get Noticed

I try to train each morning outside, but in the depths of winter it can become tough for the vehicles to see me. With the dark snowy stormy mornings of a Rocky Mountain winter engulfing our community, it takes a different approach to get noticed. Now, I decorate myself like a Christmas tree to try and get the cars racing down the icy streets to see me.

Similarly in life, I have tried to focus on skills and abilities that I offer which set me apart from others. It is key to understand these skills, hone them and keep them front of mind in the market or with your employer.

So put your own Christmas lights on–in whatever shape they may take–you may have unique ideas or concepts, you may be able to create a public relations campaign better than others, or are a math whiz and can complete a tax return in no time flat. Do what makes you shine and work at excelling at your strengths.

* * * *

39. Leverage Your Stage in Life to Move Forward

I often get asked, "How do you do it?"

First, I make the most out of life and work. I view my work as my passion, so it's easy to commit time and enthusiasm towards it.

Second, I see my job as my "stage". It's not just asking about getting tasks or actions done, but about making the most out of what I'm doing so that I can create the greatest value for my team, my company and myself.

If you view your work as "I'll just get done what needs to be done" or "I only do what is required", then you are not making the most out of your time and energy. You have to change "work" and view it as your "stage".

Once you see yourself as being on a stage, you have to decide how you would like people to view you. What do you want people to see? Like most, you want to do your best, no matter what you do. If you work in customer service, use this stage for engaging people, learn how to provide excellent service, share your spirit and perhaps allow that person to have a better day. Leverage your best skills and bring your A-game to whatever you do.

* * * *

40. A Mountain of Effort and No One Notices

People love to hear about the pain, effort and sacrifice you went through if you can tell your story in a way that gets the audience engaged. At the time of writing this, a challenge for me was getting out the door on a daily basis in the most extreme of Alberta's winter weather. I knew how important it was to train in conditions that would simulate what we would experience in the Yukon.

But this is no simple task. As co-coordinator of a busy family, VP of Marketing at Canada's largest ski resort operator and a busy travel and social schedule, training and preparation can get forgotten.

Never forget that there is an audience out there that listens to you and is a follower of you. Make sure that you keep them engaged. Don't worry about the ones that aren't listening. Keep building your brand value with the fans that care and listen.

If you are a small business operator, you need your core audience (the ones who care) to keep you in business. Keep telling them engaging stories, and they will spread your word. The power of word of mouth can be incredible. Stay focused on telling your story to your listeners and don't worry about those that don't want to hear it. Get your listeners engaged in climbing your daily or monthly mountain.

* * * *

41. If You Have Naysayers, Turn Them Into Your Partners

At one time or another, everyone has to work on teams. Sometimes, those teams can drag us down. A simple way to get naysayers on your side is to engage them in your project early on. Send them a briefing on your concept, idea or plan. Ask them point blank to provide feedback or input on how the project can be made better or enhanced. Try this the next time you have a project. You need the team to endorse it. Listen to their feedback and input carefully, and you'll quickly turn critics into collaborators and likely gain some valuable input on your project as well.

* * * *

DREAM ATTAINMENT

42. Don't Hold Back- Ask For It!

I have asked for every great opportunity that life has afforded me. Don't hold back. If you want to do something, you have to be the one reaching for it! Ask for that pay raise, ask for that new job, ask for a date if you're single and you've met someone who is amazing. Don't hold back. The only issue you will have is the feelings of "I wish I did", "I should have done that" or "I could have".

Don't give yourself the chance to have any of the "I wish", "I should" or "I could" regrets. Just go out and ask for it! Remember that sometimes you need to give yourself a kick in the ass because sometimes we get complacent as we get older. Or, conversely sometimes once we have seen some success we think we have "done enough" and don't have to ask for more. Don't fall into this trip—be humble, know what you want and don't be afraid to ask for it.

* * * *

43. Aim for the Exceptional

When I participate in wilderness adventure trips, I am not the best at being creative in the camp kitchen, nor am I the fastest hiker, paddler or biker. It's not that I don't like eating good food—I do! But I know that cooking isn't my best talent so I often refer to guidebooks or other members of the team to select food for our trips. Similarly, I am not always first into the camp. I'm not always the fastest or the one in the best shape. But I can navigate, I have a strong intuition in nature, am determined and I have a positive attitude. These are the traits that I focus on being exceptional at fostering. All of us have talents. Identify and focus on your talents and become exceptional at them.

* * * *

44. Be Better, Be Different

The worlds of sport and business can be very competitive. There are millions of people and hundreds of thousands of companies doing the same thing. How can you compete in this cluttered, high speed, over-stimulated world? I am convinced that if you are fueled by your passion and drive, work hard and practice your trade/art for over 10,000 hours and hone yourself to be the very best, then you will succeed. You also have to focus on what you do so that it is unique and different and sets you apart from the masses.

* * * *

45. Little Steps Make a Big Difference in the Long Run

Big things can only be achieved if you focus day in and day out on little steps. In writing this book, I had to focus on getting into the habit of writing something every day or I would have never finished it.

In the workplace, if you have meetings with your team, you have to make sure you consistently have the meeting on the same day each week or the meetings will not happen. You cannot skip the meetings either or the chain of habit quickly becomes broken. It can be easy to skip out of routine but easy to keep it once it becomes habit. Doing something in a small way each day is what makes any of life's projects possible to be completed in the long run.

While training for the Yukon Challenge, we started training 65 days before the event with a running plan to build up our cardio strength. The plan laid out training milestones for us each week, and it was critical to do what was required for each of those specific days. Each day built up our cardio foundation so that we would be able to run the half marathon and snowshoe climb up a mountain during the Challenge. Life, whether it's sport, family or business, requires lots of little steps to make sure that you achieve your goals. In family, it is about consistently sharing trust, care and respect each week to create building blocks within the family. Share stories from your life and demonstrate core values to your kids and repeat this over and over again. Hundreds of small steps done right will lead you to success in family, life and business.

* * * *

46. A Swirl of Activity Does Not Make Success

Sometimes, slowing down and thinking what you are going to do will produce better results. In the Yukon, when it's minus 30 degrees outside, it is better to slow down and try and do what exactly is needed to succeed.

Now, you can freeze your tutu off if you don't get your tent or shelter constructed in a timely fashion, but if you hurry too quickly you may also waste (much needed) energy and in the end the consequences of not having your shelter up quickly can become disastrous. So, slow down and perform the required tasks with skill and thought and in the end you will actually get your results faster and most importantly, safely. Fast and furious don't create success. Planned, organized and properly executed tasks will help garner greater success.

* * * *

47. I Don't Mean…Don't Hustle

Ok, so being organized and meticulous doesn't mean that you shouldn't give your best effort, or try and perform tasks quickly when time is of the essence.

If you see an opportunity and don't act quickly enough, you sometimes will not reap the benefit. So, you need always have a plan at the ready and then execute that plan quickly. Following the plan and giving it your hustle and energy will give you the advantage over others who take their time to seize an opportunity.

I once took a trip where I had planned to climb a peak in a remote wilderness park. Prior to starting the trip, we checked the weather, and it looked good. We planned to go in a certain way, climb the peak and return out on the same route. One member of our group recommended that we check alternative routes and review them in advance, just in case we needed an escape route due to possible inclement weather.

Others in the group weren't worried about a plan B as the weather was perfect at the time so we didn't bother to make other plans. However, unknown to us, one member took the time to review alternate route options and the time it would take to travel each of them.

We climbed all day, and in fact the route we had planned for took a lot longer than expected. Large car-sized boulders can be fun to play on but when you have 1,000 of them strewn across your route it can be very tough going. Very slow travel ensued for our group.

After a full day, we finally reached the peak in the early evening. Before we reached the pinnacle of the summit, we felt rushing air and colder temperatures. To our shock, we peered around the top of the rock and saw a big black swirling cloud bank rushing our way with what looked to be a northern express storm with snow and high winds. We knew we had to hurry but we also knew we would be in trouble if we hustled without a plan.

Fortunately, the one member who took the time to preview and consider other return routes had a quick solution and outlined a plan for us. His plan took us to a protected Alpine basin before nightfall. We had to hustle to get there but since we had a pre-planned route already mapped out, we were able to quickly dec5ide our direction of travel before the storm and nightfall set in. We were able to get off the peak and to our return destination safely.

* * * *

48. Seeing is Believing

This is an easy one but very profound. Want to see something amazing? Write a list of everything that you have accomplished in your life so far. Know that you have already done so much. Then, write the list of what you want to accomplish. Keep this list in a place that you see regularly. Focus on the top goals and create the steps you need to accomplish to achieve your goal and start working on each of them.

* * * *

49. Three Keys

I'd like to share three keys with you to help you build success. But first, review your accomplishments at least once a year–you will be impressed! You're doing it!

You're making it happen! You are somebody! Read it, feel it and be proud of yourself. Now, if you see some gaps between where you were and where you would like to be, draw awareness to that and make a plan to get started. Don't dwell on excuses you can make, like "I needed more education", "I didn't have time", etc. Just get started and make your way towards your goal. Celebrate what you have done and make a plan to address what you haven't accomplished.

Three keys to success that you can always be working on include:

1) Build and Maintain Strong Friendships and Relationships

Communicate daily with a key relationship. This could be a co-worker who you find inspirational to you. Surround yourself with success. It could be a friend who has gained much success in their life or art, business or family and spend time watching, asking questions and listening. You will learn ideas, tips and input that will enhance your life. You need friends who challenge you to be your best, who support your quest to reach for the stars and who won't cut you down when you face challenges.

The social time spent with quality friends is high value for you professionally but also for your mind and spirit. On the flipside, don't spend time with people who are lazy, apathetic or who appear unmotivated.

Make sure you spend time with people who share the same values as you. Gossipers, people without dreams or who are unkind are not worth spending time with and can be detrimental to your wellbeing! Spend your time wisely.

2) Work hard and don't give up. The 10,000 hour rule counts.

10,000 hours to become a master? It's true. There are so many examples of people who have written books for more than 10 years and never have one published until year 11. Toiling year after year on a project of your dreams is not easy. It can take its toll on your finances, your family and your relationships and it can take its toll on you. You can lose faith in your abilities, and you may stop going to parties and socials as you can't bear to hear another "When is your book coming out?" or "Have you been published yet?" This can be a tough time. But look at this time as the training, practice and refinement of skills that will help you to build, create and deliver something great. Enjoy the journey.

3) Believe in yourself. Optimism works!

If the constant thought running through your mind is "I will do this" then you can skip this section. But I have a feeling that each person has a shred of doubt running through their minds at some point. All positive, optimistic people share a core belief–they know that they can create value for others.

We have all been around the person that always says "that will never work" when a new idea is proposed. Many current successful leaders have had to deal with countless rejections–politicians lose election battles, inventors have botched prototypes, the consummate salesman doesn't get the deal. Not only did these leaders need a good concept, but the common driving force is that successful people believe that they can positively do something, that they can create value. Having this positive view helps them to never give up. Having an optimistic outlook helps them keep at it when the going gets tough and helps them see opportunity when others never will. So how can you become more optimistic? Have "positive" thoughts at the tip of your tongue, all the time, for yourself and for others.

* * * *

Welcome to Muktuk Adventures "a place for people who love dogs"

I am drawn to special places — like Muktuk Adventures — we share the love of Dogs!

* * * *

SELF TRANSFORMATION

50. Challenge Yourself

Beyond all of the great benefits (mind, body and spirit) for engaging in adventure, the associated benefits of pursuing a goal towards a longer term adventure activity are significant.

Your mind functions better when you have goals that challenge you each day. If you don't have something you are working towards, it is easier for the mind to drift and negative thoughts may creep back in. Setting a goal towards an adventure activity challenges you and will help you to grow.

To keep plants thriving in a garden, you need to add nutrients and turn the soil. Similarly, in life we need to maintain activity and adventure. If you are not "turning your soil" through physical and mental activity regularly, you can get stale. This is particularly true in northern climates, where there is less natural sunlight in the winter. Getting outside is critical to your health.

* * * *

51. Today is Cold and Snowy- Take Time to Play, Replay and Review

Don't run, the snow is too deep, the wind is too strong, the clouds are too threatening. Canadian Rocky Mountain snowstorms hammered the plains in 2010. On many days, the temperature hovered around minus twelve Celsius and with the wind chill, it felt more like minus twenty. Some winter mornings we are meant to be indoors.

Pour yourself a cup of your favorite hot inspiration to get your mind firing and start your day. Start with good energy foods to be ready for action in the morning. I have one cup of coffee, banana and oatmeal at the start of every day. As you know, I get up early. For me, 4:30 a.m. is a wonderful time to collect my thoughts and organize my day.

Give yourself some time to think about projects you are working on or would like to work on and then plan the road map for your day.

Treat your body as well as you treat your mind. Don't load up on sugar filled breakfast cereals. Have a piece of fruit, steel cut oatmeal and two eggs to combine a magic fuel mix for your system. Take the early morning time to yourself to review your personal and professional goals, define your next steps to keep the project moving forward. Work on the short term tasks (that week and next week) and also review the status and progress of key longer term projects (that month or next month) so that you know that progress is being made.

* * * *

52. Never Give Up

When your windows are frozen shut and your ice-encrusted thermometer is giving you a number so far to the negative that it is more than your age, it is hard to get out the door for a run or a workout. Setting an adventure commitment will help you stay on course, because you have a goal, and you need to stick to it. Relentlessly pursue your goals. Being able to stay on track and never giving up is one of the major keys to lifelong success in anything you pursue.

So, how do you do it when your mind and the weather are giving you excuses not to go outside for that workout? Simply put the gear and clothes on and step out the door. Bypass your mind with action and you will succeed. "Go and Do" when your mind is saying "Stay and Stop".

* * * *

53. Whispers in Your Ear

Trust your inner thoughts. I'm sure you can think of multiple experiences where you have experienced this before. At one time, on a very tough and dangerous whitewater trip part of our team selected a location to put in the boat. I was having second thoughts when I was looking at the maps. I thought we were too far up the river and that particular location might put us into some class four or five rapids. The rest of the team agreed to put in at that location and in a very short time, our lives were in jeopardy, as we could hear the roar of a waterfall ahead and the river had picked up so much speed that we were fully committed to run it. I watched in complete horror as one of our boats in front completely disappeared into the certain death trap in front of us. Fortunately the boat popped back up and everyone was okay.

You get these voices or instincts talking to you all the time—whether it's when you're walking down a dark street late at night, a questionable restaurant in a foreign country, going hiking and needing to make a decision about which trail to take, or sitting in a job interview and feeling that the prospective company just isn't the right fit for you. Learn to listen and trust your intuition. Honing that skill will allow you to make better decisions and hopefully keep you away from some sticky situations.

* * * *

54. Hang with the Right Pack

Get with the right dog team and you can win the race. That's what I learned on the Yukon Challenge. It comes from caring for the dogs, surviving in a harsh climate and committing to each other, that you will never give up. A positive attitude is critical when working with your dog team, as the dogs have senses that are more acute than humans, and they can tell if you really care about them. Similarly in life, remember that the friends you hang with in life help create and join you on the race called life. Surround yourself with good people and you will have a great time in life. We have all been there, where we've been with the wrong people. Remember the trips or experiences that were dampened by their company. The right people can make or break each step of your journey.

* * * *

55. Go the Distance

During one canoe trip into the wilds of northern British Columbia, we encountered a situation where we had to make a decision. It was late on a stormy night, and we were trying to find a good campsite, when we came across a cabin after a long portage of a section of waterfalls. We were completely soaked and very cold. In what looked like a mirage in the distance, an old trapper's cabin appeared in front of us. Sometimes on long journeys involving serious physical and mental workouts you can start to see things that you would like to have appear so I pinched myself (which is what I do during these extreme situations when I want my mind to correct itself as to what is real) and to my amazement, the cabin was still there. Allow me to put this into perspective for you–finding a cabin in the middle of northern British Columbia when you dearly need one is like winning the lottery.

We stepped out of our water-laden canoes and onto the deep soft sandy beach. Normally, you would feel the oozing water-soaked mud as it fills up your river shoes but by now we could not even feel our feet since they were so cold.

One monster mud-sucking step at a time, we reached the front door of the early 1900s cabin. On the front door was a hand written note held in place by a very large knife. We read it slowly out loud, "Don't stay here, large bear roams night and day". It went on, "Want to know how big–check out the smashed-in window. Prior to the bear's arrival there was a steel-barred window that would have kept out a large truck at ramming speed".

We ventured to the side of the cabin and saw bear tracks in the sand. Their immense size dwarfed our river shoes when we stepped into the foot print. We took heed to the notice and decided to go the distance. We knew we had to travel further down the river and get to a place that would provide some safety from a potentially very dangerous bear.

Make a commitment to always go the distance and make the last mile very important. Finish brilliantly whatever you are doing.

* * * *

56. Minus 37- Open Your Door and Your Life Will Be Better

The day was November 23. It wasn't even winter yet but it was so cold in Calgary that day, that only an Antarctic weather station was reporting colder temperatures—we were the second coldest place on the planet!

For many, the topic of the weather is a conversation centre piece at the office, in the coffee shops and around town. It starts with, "This weather sucks" or "this weather has really got me down". You can't change the weather but you can change how you let it affect you.

Back to that bitter cold morning—there wasn't much wind but just enough that it cut through the high tech layers of my clothing, reminding me that I would need more layers for the Yukon.

It was warm inside, and I could have just stayed there, enjoying the newspaper and a strong cup of coffee. But drive comes from pushing yourself—your inside fire needs to burn strong and ignite your passion to excel in life.

My drive was flickering that day. It is normal to have days of flickering, but this is where true growth, strength and never giving up takes over. Your adventure, whatever it may be, will be hard at work enhancing and challenging your life's normal routine. Open the door (literally or figuratively) and your life will be better for it. On that particular morning, it was quiet out. Christmas lights were on but the air was so cold I had a hard time focusing on my surroundings.

Commitment is about stepping one foot out while your mind makes a last ditch effort to retract your leg and tells you, "Don't do it. Are you crazy?" Remove these thoughts and with a swift action, kick the other leg out. My challenge that morning came in the form of my three year old golden retriever, who put one paw out then hightailed it back to the warm blankets on the couch. I wanted my furry partner in crime with me and thankfully he loyally rejoined my side after a friendly beckoning.

About forty minutes into the run I am starting to feel the real threats of the weather. In this cold environment the sounds are so harsh and rough–it is like a bunch of kids constantly running their finger nails down the chalkboard. It's lonely and you are not only in a situation where you are not comfortable but in these temperatures anything you do outside can be dangerous. I pay attention to my exposed skin as I begin to feel the early stages of frostbite.

In the cold and dark your mind can also become easily sidetracked to dark and negative thoughts. "What if I fall, what if I don't make it back home, what am I doing here?" But you do it. You push through your preset normal day or routine of life, and you begin to grow by pushing your way through challenges. You start to learn more about yourself and what you can accomplish. With practice, as you start to receive negative thoughts, you can now push them out and improve your mindset. You start to create a positive outlook for yourself in very demanding situations. Your adventure has started, as it is changing your view and enhancing your life.

* * * *

57. Seeing is Believing

It can be a tough thing to see your family and friends for who they are and not for whom they once were or who they aren't. It's not easy. Particularly when it comes to your children. It can be hard to see them for whom they are and not for whom you want them to be. But it's critical for their own development and self worth that they be nurtured and encouraged to forge their own paths and become whom they are and whom they want to be.

Some of their turns in life and their interests can sometimes go against your interests or desires for them– such as if your kids start wearing clothes that are just plain strange or they decide they want to become a rapper. Provided your kids aren't harming themselves, keep your cool and wade through these stages. Kids will find their rudder and eventually learn to correct their path. If they know that they have your trust, support and confidence to allow them to be who they want to be will provide them with the greatest strength they can be provided. Support and guidance will give a significant boost to their self confidence and it builds the bond you can share with your kids.

Be a coach from the sidelines and let them explore different opportunities; they'll decide what path they are meant to take and will find their way.

* * * *

58. Review Your Challenges, but Don't Dwell on Mistakes

Some simple steps can be taken to enhance your lowest star skills. I have many areas that I need to work on, so I try to focus on those areas and then enlist support from close friends to help provide me with honest input. This can be difficult for some but instead of dodging criticism, learn to embrace it. Treat input as a means of building your skills and work on it.

Review some of your past successes and reflect on what you did that made a difference. Never stop learning and use each challenge as a valuable learning experience.

* * * *

59. Do What You Think You Can't

Don't listen to them. Many will doubt that you are capable of achieving greatness. However, there is only one person you need to convince to start the march for greatness and that person is you.

Set your sights high, aim far and then begin one step at a time. Don't take detours; believe that you can make it, even during the toughest times. Taking one step at a time is critical. Don't focus on what it will be like when you reach your goal but focus on each small step along the way and celebrate as you accomplish each small step. It is a progression and it is a long journey. Enjoy the path versus thinking all will only be good once you reach the end. This approach will give you the optimism that you need to stay positive through any adversity.

* * * *

60. People Will Not Always "Get" You

Don't give up and constantly repeat your message. I have a blog and I also often conduct media interviews. Sometimes, people misread or misunderstand what I'm articulating. Words can be taken out of context or misconstrued. Dwelling on this kind of negativity can quickly get under your skin. But don't let it bother you. You have to move forward and continue to tell your story. Every brand needs repetition to get noticed, including your own personal brand. Believe in your values and articulate yourself well.

* * * *

61. Positive Words

Watch what you say to others. Think before you talk. All of the cliché sayings really do have meaning. Positive self-talk is not only important but also when you are having conversations with others, particularly when you meet people for the first time. People judge others within a very short amount of time. Be positive with kind words, inspiration and create good conversations.

People intuitively know who they enjoy talking with and who has made a lasting impression on them. Doors open for those who make a positive impact on those they meet. It may sound strange but people buy other people. The more positive you bring out both in yourself and in others, the more that opportunities will come your way.

* * * *

62. Look At What's Right in Front of You

Sometimes we get stuck trying to find a new idea; trying to come up with the market-beating new concept. Sometimes the best opportunity can be right in front of you.

Make sure to take the time and look at what you already do, what you have already done and what capabilities you already possess. Focus on yourself and building more value on the skills, connections or attributes you already have.

I work in the ski industry, a place where we have lots of fun events for our guests. What we noticed was that on certain weekends, attendance at certain events was flat. We could have gone back to the drawing board and created an entirely new event but that process comes at a greater expense and a potential for a loss of brand awareness that comes from a long running event. So, we looked at it from the perspective of what we could add or do to the existing event to create a greater draw and enhance the guests' experiences.

To create greater value in life, don't just look at new ideas but also take a look at what's right in front of you for inspiration.

* * * *

63. Be an Agent of Positive Change at Work

You will have people who just don't understand that having a positive attitude not only will improve their life but will also enhance their work excperience. Work hard to be the agent of change at your workplace, in your daily life, at home or with your friends. Always be yourself and share a positive attitude. Read situations and understand where to apply your efforts that will help use your time and energy to your best advantage. The key is to be willing to make a difference in all of your environments– work, home and play.

* * * *

I'd like to leave you with a few important thoughts. You have likely heard this before, but I don't think we can ever hear it enough: We only go through this life once and remember there is no handbook, so make it a point to make each and every day count. Even when you're tired, facing unexpected challenges, facing constant failure, or when you feel hurt or embarrassed, these are the curve balls of life and it can be hard to see out of the eye of the storm.

Add adventure to your Life. Daily. Stick to it. Remember it can be as simple as "Dance Nude, Sing and Play Games" or a walk in that nearby park. Stick to it, even when your friends and family are questioning what you are doing. It is key, as long as you are not hurting anyone, to stick to your inner compass. Add Adventure, explore your inner child and get outside regularly.

Famous last words. Every step will not be easy and to get the most from your life you will face challenges.

Always remember that the challenge has been given to you because you are capable of dealing with it, of turning it into a positive. At first you may not see the positive.

But always try your best, have a positive attitude and persevere through the challenge and the pain as best you can because on the other side there will be something of benefit for you. No one can tell you what that is. But if you face your challenges with negative energy you will not find the positive. From the challenging door you will move forward (sometimes hard and slow) but keep at it as there will be a positive door that will open for you. You have to believe in this. Never give up, enjoy your adventures each day and always think positively. You make a difference in this world!

* * * *

A special place to camp where the Peaks meet the Valley

* * * *

THE ADVENTURER'S GUIDE TO LIVING A HAPPY LIFE

ABOUT THE AUTHOR

Matt Mosteller, known as Powder Matt, one of North America's top Ski Bloggers, shares his passion for the mountains & skiing with a bunch of remarkable, like minded people at one of North America's largest private mountain resort operators, Resorts of the Canadian Rockies. An avid Adventurer, travel writer, author, professional speaker, professional ski coach, whitewater guide, fly fishing guide and Hollywood private ski guide and what many of his friends will confirm a certified health nut–who eats grass for lunch. Why not have Powder Matt speak at your next event as he loves to share his thoughts on leading a 'Happy Life', Celebrating 'Goose Bump Moments'. He is often found skiing Fernie, British Columbia and trying to keep up with his wife and 2 kids.

* * * *

ACKNOWLEDGEMENTS & GRATITUDE

No one is self-taught. It takes a team to make it in life. I am fortunate to have a great team. I may be at fault here like many of us for not giving enough credit to this great team, and I apologize profusely in advance if I leave anyone out. As I wrote this note, while out in the wilderness with my hands shaking in fear, and after conquering one class 4, ass chewing, bone crushing rapid and a whitewater rapid number two coming up shortly; I was facing my fear of swimming one rapid at a time....

Passion (some people refer to this as job and/or work) is what you really get excited about. It is what your life is all about. High in the Canadian Rockies, at one of the ski resorts along the famed powder highway, I was fortunate to give a tour and share my passion for the mountains and skiing. I was in my trusted oldie but goodie 1976 Toyota Landcruiser, complete with rusted out floorboards, doors that locked on their own and windows that would neither go up and or down. This person, unbeknownst to me, would become my business mentor. We bonded. I got a new role, and I am still getting my MBA (Murray's Business Admin degree). I am extremely grateful for all the guidance, leadership and coaching that Murray Edwards and Larry Moeller have provided me. Most importantly, I treasure the friendship that I have shared with Murray, his amazing wife Heather and Larry Moeller.

I am also surrounded by a very talented and capable team at the resorts of the Canadian Rockies. It is truly an honor to be part of this team.

Life Adventures. From early beginnings, exploring the backwoods with a good buddy, Dan Evans, sparked an interest in Adventure. Going outside was fun. Skiing came sliding into my life and brought one great road trip after another. But for being such an individual sport, it showed me how much you depend on others along the way....from places to stay, carpool rides to get to the mountains and pot-lucks (where was the next meal coming from?). Thanks to Chris Shaw, Bruce Foster, Debbie Armstrong, Ingrid, Leroy Kingland, Alex Murray, Sturtevants, Olympic Sports, Ron Steele, Charlie Dresen, Jeff Pickering, Dave Culp and many others. Ski racing to rowing crew- Ouch!? Yeah that is what my body said. Trying to change fast twitch muscles to a leaner cardio machine was not a great success for me. But this sport clearly shows the importance of teamwork and is all about hardwork and discipline. From this sport came many friends. I was very fortunate to be able to spend time with Mike Filippone and Greg Kapust.

Back to the Rocky Mountains for more Outdoor Adventures: ski race coaching, ski trips, fly fishing, canoe trips, whitewater adventures, climbing and long arduous backpacking trips with great friends Don Long, Andy Feury, Becky Lomax (she has fed me almost more than anyone and has the biggest heart full of care! Thank you for all your support with writing and life!), George Widener, former US Senator Al Simpson, Paul Mahre, Todd Scott, Jikke Stegeman, Jim Nielson, Ted Allsopp, Al Charest, Don Bell, Pat Bates, Frank Ackerman, Wally & Sandy Ganzi, Michael O'Connor, Mike Delich, Max Gartner, Chris Slubicki, Michael Lang, Bill Dejong, Glen Gradeen, Stuart O'Connor, Don Olsson family, Bruce & Tyler Erickson, Dick Hughes, Dan Nordstrom and many others.

Life begins at the end of your comfort zone. For this I am grateful to have spent quality time, laughs and journeys with Gordon & Marion Dixon (you guys are amazing, full of care, love, fun and 'great life input'!!), Gord Martin, Jim Mcintyre, (Jim & Gord cheers to many more wacky and zany adventures. You guys rock!) and Bobby Model. I was very fortunate to have spent time with this worldwide adventurer who shared his positive spirit and energy with everyone he came in contact with, and although he had more adventures in his short lifetime than many would ever dream of, his passing was like a bat hitting my head reminding me to constantly hug/love your family and friends.

My first book. Paula Worthington, Becky Lomax for helping me out with writing and providing support and care. Hutch Morton, thank you for believing in me and for being the best publisher that an author could have! The Team at Premier Digital Publishing! You guys are great and I appreciate all the extra effort and support! Gordon Wiltsie, National Geographic Photographer and Laura Munson, author extraordinaire, your kind words of support made all the difference!

Family is the engine room of team. I am very fortunate and blessed to have a loving and caring family. I am very thankful for friendship and support of the whole Murphy gang (Tim & family). I dedicate this book to my wife, two kids and my dog. Mom, Dad and Brother Bob, the foundation of care, love and friendship for always listening and supporting my dreams from the beginning.

I want to thank my family for all their love, support and for creating a positive environment for where hope can propel you above experience, and chasing your dreams is the norm.

-Matt Mosteller

* * * *

CPSIA information can be obtained at www.ICGtesting.com
Printed in the USA
LVOW101830260613

340375LV00013B/540/P